FASTER, SLOWER, HIGHER, LOWER

By Michael Berenstain

A GOLDEN BOOK • NEW YORK

Western Publishing Company, Inc., Racine, Wisconsin 53404

Faster,

slower,

higher,

lower.

2

Bigger,

smaller,

taller.

shorter,

3

Over,

under,

around

and through.

Up and down,

many, few.

5

Open,

shut,

out

and in.

6

Top,

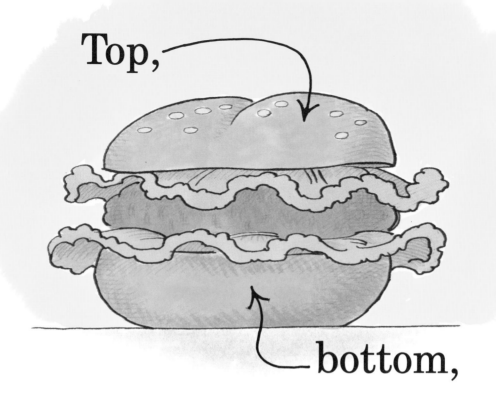

bottom,

thick

and thin.

7

8

9

Here, there,

short, long.

10

Hard,   soft,

strong.

weak,

11

Floating,

sinking,

wet and dry.

13

far,

Near,

shallow,

deep.

14

Noisy,

quiet,

awake,

asleep.

Sick, healthy,

happy, sad.

Neat,   messy,

good,   bad.

17

On,   off,

dark,

light.

Wide,

narrow,

loose,

tight.

Warm,

cool,

hot,

cold.

Plain, fancy,

old.

young,

Blunt,

sharp,

smooth,

rough.

22

Sweet,   sour,

tender,   tough.

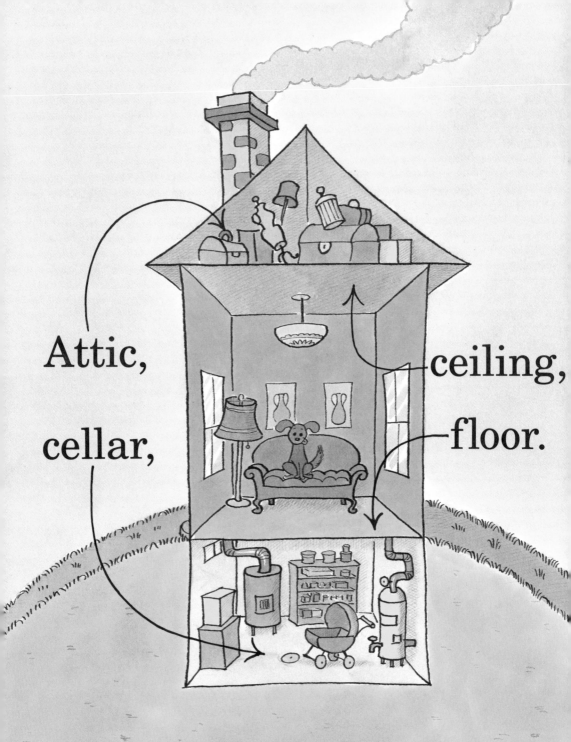

Attic,

cellar,

ceiling,

floor.

24

Huge
and
tiny,

less and more.

Forward,

backward,

flat,

bumpy.

Hero,

villain,

cheerful,

grumpy.

Apart,   together,

push and pull.

Frozen, melted,

empty, full.

29

receive and send.

Early,   late,

beginning . . .

end.

DUE DATE

			Printed in USA